Łukasz Gładysiak • Grzegorz Okoński •

Sturmgeschütz IV

KAGERO

Kagero Publishing would like to thank the following people

Mr Grzegorz Okoński and Mr Jacek Szafrański, through whom posting of *Sturmgeschütz IV* from Rgilewka River photos was possible. Separate thanks we would like to send to the Museum of Armoured Weapon of the Army Training Centre in Poznań as well as the Museum of Armaments, Wielkopolska Museum of Independence Campaigns in Poznań for sharing elements of their collections.

Sturmgeschütz IV • Łukasz Gładysiak, Grzegorz Okoński, Jacek Szafrański • First edition • LUBLIN 2014

© All English Language Rights Reserved. With the exception of quoting brief passages for the purposes of review, no part of this publication may be reproduced without prior written permission from the Publisher. Nazwa serii zastrzeżona w UP RP • ISBN 978-83-64596-20-9

Editors: **Marek Jaszczołt** • Translation: **Jarosław Dobrzyński** • Color profiles: **Arkadiusz Wróbel** • 3D rendering: **Tomasz Idzikowski** • Design: **KAGERO STUDIO, Marcin Wachowicz**

Oficyna Wydawnicza KAGERO
Akacjowa 100, Turka, os. Borek, 20-258 Lublin 62, Poland, phone/fax: (+48) 81 501 21 05
www.kagero.pl • e-mail: kagero@kagero.pl, marketing@kagero.pl
w w w . k a g e r o . p l

Dismounting of the *Sturmgeschütz IV* main armament – *7,5 cm StuK 40 L/48* gun using the 2-tonne load capacity crane. The crane-sockets were installed on the superstructure from June 1944. [Bundesarchiv]

Experience of fighting on the Eastern Front, especially in the face of the loss of the strategic initiative by the Third Reich in the summer of 1943 significantly influenced the development of key vehicle types of the *Panzerwaffe*. In the course of time the assault guns, originally intended only for infantry support evolved into universal combat vehicles. This situation questioned the purpose of the production of medium tanks in Germany. One of the vehicles, which at least in theory could replace them, was the *Sturmgeschütz IV.*

Design development

The history of the assault gun based on the chassis of the *Panzerkampfwagen IV* medium tank begins in the early days of 1943. At that time the representatives of the Reich's Ministry of Armaments and Ammunition recommended the development of a new version of the *Sturmgeschütz* based on the aforementioned chassis. The main argument for this idea was the reduction of the weight of the vehicles fitted with a turret and sim-

Early production series *Sturmgeschütz IVs* of *SS-Panzer-Abteilung 4.* **during the German military parade in Thessaloniki, April 1944. Despite installing frames, the** *Schürzen* **protective screens are absent. [Bundesarchiv]**

plification and hence – acceleration of the production. Besides the components planned for use, especially the drive systems were produced in large numbers per month. In February the official order was submitted to *Krupp-Grusson Aktiengesellschaft* consortium of Magdeburg. Shortly after the first design drawing, numbered *W 1468* was presented. The vehicle designated

Gerät 820, was based on *Panzerkampfwagen IV Ausf. G* (type: 9/BW) chassis. The superstructure was developed by conversion of the variant fitted to *Sturmgeschütz III Ausf. F/8* guns, delivered *Daimler-Motoren-Gesellschaft* factory of Stuttgart-Untertürkheim. Its characteristic feature was the lengthened forward section which was slanting and reached the edge of

Sturmgeschütz IV **of the German 34**[th] **Infantry Division destroyed somewhere in Italy. The vehicle represents the second half of 1944 production series based on** *Panzerkampfwagen IV Ausf. G/H* **chassis. [Bundesarchiv]**

Sturmgeschütz IVs belong to *SS-Panzer-Abteilung 4.*, during the Thessaloniki military parade. All photographed vehicles represents the early production series with *Zimmerit* coating applied between January and September 1944. [Bundesarchiv]

the *bathtub*. According to the guidelines the front armor was to be 80 mm thick and the side armor – 45 – 50 mm. The main armament was the *7,5 cm Sturmkanone 40* gun with the barrel length of 48 calibers. The vehicle's weight was up to 22,260 kg.

Although it was envisaged that the new tracked vehicle would replace the *Panzerkampfwagen IV* tanks in the future, its introduction to series production took almost a year. The change of the attitude of the decision makers in Berlin was influenced by the battle of Kursk fought in July of 1943. Losses

suffered during this battle, especially the loss of the strategic initiative on the Eastern Front by the Third Reich caused that since then the Panzerwaffe was rather to operate in defensive conditions. This coincidence favored assault guns, proven many times even in extreme conditions, especially versions armed with long – barreled 75-mm guns.

Between 19 and 22 August of 1943 Adolf Hitler had a series of meetings with representatives of the officer corps, during which the significant role of the assault guns, especially in op-

US Army soldiers posing on the roof of *Sturmgeschütz IV* destroyed by the allied troops in Western Europe or Italy. The *Zimmerit* protective layer is clearly visible. On this vehicles it was applied between January and September 1944. [Bundesarchiv]

Another photo of *Sturmgeschütz IV* of *SS-Panzer-Abteilung 4.* exhibited in Thessaloniki, in April 1944. Later presented vehicles were probably sent to the Italian front. [Bundesarchiv]

Destroyed in Italy *Sturmgeschütz IV* of the German 34th Infantry Division presented on page 4 photographed from another angle. There is a 2-tonne crane socket visible on the right side of presented exemplar. The right-side *Schürzen* protective screens frame is missing. [Bundesarchiv]

Sturmgeschütz IV of Amoured Weapon Museum in Poznań during its recovering from Rgilewka river near Grzegorzew in Poland, Jyly 2006. The massive gun mantlet and 75 mm caliber barrel are clearly visible. [Grzegorz Okoński]

erations conducted on the expanses of the Eastern Front. The direct stimulus for starting the assembly of the *Sturmgeschütz IV* was the November bombing of the *Altmärkische Kettenfabrik* factory, the main manufacturer of the *Sturmgeschütz III Ausf. G*, which had affected badly the further production of this type. Despite the damages of the assembly halls it was possible to complete the prototype of the body intended to be mounted on the chassis of the standard German medium tank. It was a modification of the equivalent fitted to the most popular version of the assault gun – the change consisted in moving the position of the driver forward, which resulted in a gap,

subsequently faired over by a sheet of steel. A similar measure was fairing over the openings in the bottom part. Obligatory decisions were made on 6 and 7 December, when the *Führer* himself opted for the commencement of completion of the latest version of the assault gun even if it was to reduce the number of the turreted vehicles sent to the front line as replacements. In this case the priority was to make up for the shortages caused by the destruction of the Berlin-Spandau factory.

On 16 December the complete prototype was showed the representatives of the army and the highest state authorities. The effect made by the display resulted in the order for 850

Recovering of *Sturmgeschütz IV* from Rgilewka river near Grzegorzew (Poland) in the summer of 2006. [Grzegorz Okoński]

Table 1. Modifications of the *Sturmgeschütz IV* with dates of introduction

	Range of modification
January 1944	Beginning of applying of Zimmerit anti-magnetic coating.
April 1944	Fitting of external machine gun. Fitting of additional gun blocking supports. Removal of bottom escape hatch.
May 1944	Fitting of Schürzen protection screens. Fitting of universal ammunition container.
June 1944	Fitting of additional armor of the drivers position. Fitting of a new type of tow hooks. Fitting of supports for folding crane on the upper plate of the superstructure. Modification of the angle of inclination of the gun barrel in the yoke.
July 1944	Fitting of the transport rack on the rear part of the upper plate of the engine compartment.
August 1944	Fitting of rotating commander's turret (some vehicles). Fitting of remote controller machine gun Fitting of smoke and fragmentation grenade launcher (some vehicles).
September 1944	Cease of applying of Zimmerit anti-magnetic coating.
October 1944	Modernization of the loader's hatch.
November 1944	Fitting of the gun barrel transit support. Fitting of raincovers of the driver's periscopes. Adaptation of tow hooks for a towbar. Modification of battery heating system. Strengthening of the lateral transmission gearbox
December	Introduction of the Panzefampfwagen IV Ausführung J chassis.

vehicles, 350 of which 350 were to roll out of the factory even before the year's end (the rest were to be delivered in January). The new vehicle was designated *7,5 cm Sturmkanone 40 L/48 auf Fahrgestell Panzerkampfwagen IV Sonderkraftfahrzeug 167.*

Sturmgeschütz IV from Grzegorzew in Poland combat compartment roof. The 9,2 cm Nahverteidigungswaffe grenade launcher is visible in the foreground. [Grzegorz Okoński]

Scouring of *Sturmgeschütz IV* from Rgilewka river superstructure elements, summer 2006. Surprisingly the original Third Reich *Balken-kreuz* national symbol was preserved. [Grzegorz Okoński]

From the beginning the vehicles were to be assembled with collective method. Proper number of the drive systems was to be provided by the vehicle's designer – the *Krupp-Gruson AG* factory of Magdeburg, the *tubs* were delivered among others by Krupp steelworks of Essen and *Eisen-Hüttenverein* w Bochum, and the superstructures – by *Brandenburgische Eisenwerke* and *Altmärkische Kettenfabrik*. The main armament was manufactured by *Wittenauer Maschinenfabruk Aktiengesellschaft* company of Berlin and the *Škoda-Werke* factory of Pilzno. The final assembly was done in the premises of the prototype maker.

The first thirty chassis were prepared by the *Nibelungenwerke* of St. Valentin. Shortly after the New Year they were sent to the Berlin – Spandau factory and then, with complete superstructures to the *Krupp-Gruson AG* factory. In the course of further production several modifications were made, resulting from the experience of the operation of the *Sturmgeschütz III Ausf. G*. They consisted mainly in the removal of redundant elements of the chassis, left due their original purpose, among others the turret drive motor, which was planned to be replaced by an ad-

ditional fuel tank or ammunition rack. On 13 March the system of mounting of the gun in the yoke was changed. A week later in the site of the Magdeburg consortium a conference, which resulted in many improvements, had taken place. The construction of the main armament base, which was additionally fitted with locking supports, was simplified, the fittings of the prism inserts of the driver's periscopes were improved, the driver's seat was changed from a fixed to adjustable one. An externally – mounted machine gun and a sheet of metal separating the ammunition container from the exhaust system were also added. During the next month the escape hatch in the bottom was removed and in May 5 to 8 millimeter thick *Schürzen* type screens were added. The beginning of the summer resulted in the strengthening of the forward section of the superstructure with 30-mm thick *Zusatzpanzerung* armor plates fixed with screws. Installation of supports for folded cranes with 2-tonne load capacity also began. In July some vehicles were fitted with a frame made of flats, welded in the rear part of the engine compartment – this way an additional load space was created. Universal ammunition

The factory-numbering 88361 discovered on the hull of *Sturmgeschütz IV* from Grzegorzew (Poland). [Grzegorz Okoński]

containers made by Krupp appeared inside. August brought an important modification in the field of additional armament; remote controlled *Rundumsfeuer* units, enabling firing without the need to get out began to replace the previous *7,92 mm Maschinengewehr 34* or *42* machine guns installed in a folding, one-piece fairings. Apart from it the fitting of the *9,2 cm Nahverteidigungswaffe* smoke and fragmentation grenade launcher was envisaged. However in practice the implementation of both elements went very slowly. Moreover, some vehicles were fitted with fully rotating upper ring of the commander's turret. In September applying of the *Zimmerit* anti-magnetic ceramic protection layer, used nearly from the beginning of the production ceased and in October the loader's hatch was modernized. At the beginning of the next to last month of the sixth year of the war on the forward part of the chassis a support stabilizing the gun barrel in transit, preventing the deregulation of the main armament assembly, modified were also catches enabling stable fitting of the towbar. In order to improve visibility in bad weather the driver's periscopes were fitted with rain covers. Inside the fuel line and lateral transmission gearbox were improved. Due to the necessity to maintain constant temperature of batteries wooden covers were added. Since then the whole unit was heated by additional blast of hot air. Significant changes were made in December 1944 along with the definitive replacement of the *9/ BW* chassis by the version used in *Panzerkampfwagen IV Ausf. J.* tanks. It was characterized primarily by three return rollers rather than four of the earlier variant and redesigned exhaust manifold. In lieu of a large, horizontally mounted cylindrical muffler with one exhaust the *Flammentöter* assembly compris-

ing two thickened tubes, called *heating funnels* by the crews was fitted. It is worth noting that sometimes this element was combined with the older variant of the drive system – an example of this solution is the vehicle preserved at the Field Crown Stefan Czarniecki Armoured Weapon Museum of the Army Training Centre in Poznań.

On 3 November 1944, the production plan of the *Sonderkraftfahrzeug 167* was accepted. In accordance to this directives between December an the beginning of the next spring 130 exemplars per month were to roll out of the Magdeburg factory. In April 1945 it was planned to complete further 100, and in May – 50. In fact, the number of all *Sturmgeschütz IVs* amounted to 1141. Majority of them – 1111 were manufactured by *Grusonwerk* plant with *Krupp* chassis (number 100001-101111. Another 30 were sent to the German army from *Alkett* (*Nibelungenwerke* chassis, numbered from 89324 to 89382).

Technical description

The powerplant of the described vehicle was the 12-cylinder, four – stroke *Maybach HL 120 TRM* engine with twin choke *Solex JFF II* (detailed data are in Table 3). The main suppliers were *Maybach Motorenwerke Friedrichshafen* and *Auto-Union Werke Wanderer* of Chemnitz. The power was 300 hp at 3,000 rpm but it was recommended not to exceed 2,600 rpm and after the first major overhaul – 2,400 rpm. The total weight of the engine block amounted to 920 kg.

Proper engine temperature was maintained by two radiators which had total area of 2.6 sq.m mounted on both sides of the rear part of the axis. Additionally two fans mounted on the right side of the engine compartment and air inlets situated on its sides, sometimes covered with plates. In winter conditions there was a possibility to increase the heat by pumping glycol from a vehicle with already running engine – for this purpose a set of special valves was used.

The engine power was transferred by a pair of Cardan shafts. Three – plate dry *Fichtel uns Sachs 120/HD* clutch and *Zahnradfabrig Aphon SSG 77* mechanical gearbox enabled the vehicle to travel with the speed of 38 km/h on road and 20 km/h in terrain. The driver selected one of seven gears (six forward and one backward) with a lever mounted to the left of the seat. Driving the vehicle was also enabled by planetary turning mechanism and Krupp – made brakes, blocking the drive wheels.

Sturmgeschütz IV recovered from Rgilewka river in Poland 75 mm caliber barrel with muzzle brake. [Grzegorz Okoński]

The characteristic *Saukopfsblende* gun mantlet of *Sturmgeschütz IV*. This one belongs to the exemplar found in Grzegorzew in Poland. [Grzegorz Okoński]

Although the total capacity of three fuel tanks was 430 l the designers restricted that during filling about 17 l of empty space should be left. A pair of fillers closed by metal caps was situated on the left side of the tub. Standard for German World War II vehicles 74-octane fuel was supplied by two *Solex* pumps. The driver selected the fuel source with switches mounted on a control panel. The average fuel consumption was about 190 /100 km, which gave the *Sturmgeschütz IV* the unrefueled range of 210 km on road and 130 km in terrain.

The majority of the units of the described vehicle was based on *Panzerkampfwagen IV Ausf. G* medium tank chassis. The drive system comprised sixteen double wheels of 470x75x660 size with rubber bandage made by *Deutsche Dunlop Gummi Compagnie Aktiengesellschaft* or *Continental,* mounted in pairs on bogies cushioned by half leaf spring (four bogies on each side). The drive sprocket with nineteen teeth arranged in two rows was located in the front and the smooth idler wheel – in the rear. In the upper part four return rollers, supporting the tracks

Inner part of *7,5 cm StuK 40 L/48* gun mounted in *Sturmgeschütz IV*. This particular is a part of the Rgilewka river exemplar recovered in 2006. [Grzegorz Okoński]

An unknown numbering and signs applied on the Grzegorzew *Sturmgeschütz IV* hull. [Grzegorz Okoński]

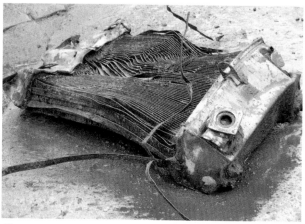

Elements of *Sturmgeschütz IV* found in Rgilewka river in Poland. [Grzegorz Okoński]

were mounted. They were usually made of steel, although some early units might be fitted with a variant with rubber bandage.

An important change in chassis took place in December 1944, when it was decided to replace previously used *9/BW* variant with the one used in *Panzerkampfwagen IV Ausf. J* tanks. It resulted primarily in reduction of the number of the return rollers to three on each side. The vehicles assembled within the last production batches might have some or all road wheels made only of steel.

On each side 99 single – bolt *Kgs 61/400/120* track shoes with a single fence, cast from manganese steel were stretched. The manufacturer - *Moorburger Treckenwerke* of Hamburg enabled fitting of anti-skid elements and broadening extensions, facilitating the movement of the vehicle on quaggy ground. In the standard variant with 400 mm width the ground pressure was 0.92 kg/cm². The length of the area of contact of the tracks with the ground was 2.52 m. On 1 May 1944 by virtue of the Directive No 256 it was recommended for the crews to replace

during the autumn/winter season the standard type of tracks with a single – element, broad variant – *Ostketten.*

The body of the *Sturmgeschütz IV* was made mostly by welding. The exception was the join with the lower parts of the vehicle, where massive angle bars and screws were used and the top of the combat compartment which was attached by the same method, which enabled quick replacement of the main armament even in field conditions. As it was mentioned at the beginning the pattern of the superstructure was taken from the assault guns based on *Panzerkampfwagen III* chassis, primarily – Type G. A departure was the cover of the driver's compartment, characteristically protruding forward, retrofitted with two periscopes.

The crew's protection consisted of heterogenic, rolled steel plates hardened by heat treatment (carbon enrichment). According to Brinnel scale their hardness reached 588 (200 kg/mm²). The thickness of the plates varied from 10 to 80 mm.

A frequent measure was makeshift strengthening of the armor, both by the *Krupp-Gruson AG* factory and the users of

Front part of the Grzegorzew *Sturmgeschütz IV* superstructure after its transportation to Armoured Weapon Museum in Poznań. Driver's periscopes covers and hatch are clearly visible as well as remnants of *Balkenkreuz* national symbol applied on the side armour. [Grzegorz Okoński]

92 mm support grenade launcher seen from outside. This one is installed on the roof of *Sturmgeschütz IV* from Grzegorzew (Poland). [Grzegorz Okoński]

Another view of the driver's compartment of Grzegorzew *Sturmgeschütz IV*. [Grzegorz Okoński]

Sturmgeschütz IV recovered from Rgilewka river in Poland superstructure photographed in 2006. Although several smaller elements were missing, the vehicle was nearly complete. [Grzegorz Okoński]

the vehicles. The most frequent method was increasing of the thickness of the cover of the driver's position and the ammunition container by addition of concrete screed. This operation was continued, despite the fact that on 24 January 1944 the General Inspector of Artillery issued an expertise which asserted that this way not only did not improve the safety but primarily brings additional dead weight. Some vehicles were also retrofitted with additional steel plated mounted at 40 or 50 degree angle on the sides and in front of the superstructure. During the last summer of the war 30-mm thick armor plates – *Zusatzpanzerung* – fitted to the front with screws were added. Until 9 September 1944 the

Zimmerit anti-magnetic ceramic coating was applied in characteristic *Riffelmuster* pattern (vertical, horizontally grooved stripes).

Basing on experience of the *Sturmgeschütz III* crews in May 1944 a decision about retrofitting the vehicles with *Schürzen* type protective screens moounted along the sides was made. In the original variant they consisted of five overlapping plates 5 to 8 mm thick (differences resulted from their origination from a certain supplier). Three plates in the middle had rectangular shape, while the first and last – trapezoid. All were suspended on a steel frame welded to three outriggers. Correct position was provided by eight triangular plates (teeth) placed

Rear plate of Grzegorzew *Sturmgeschütz IV*. The right hatch and radio antenna mounting with its rubber socket are clearly visible. [Grzegorz Okoński]

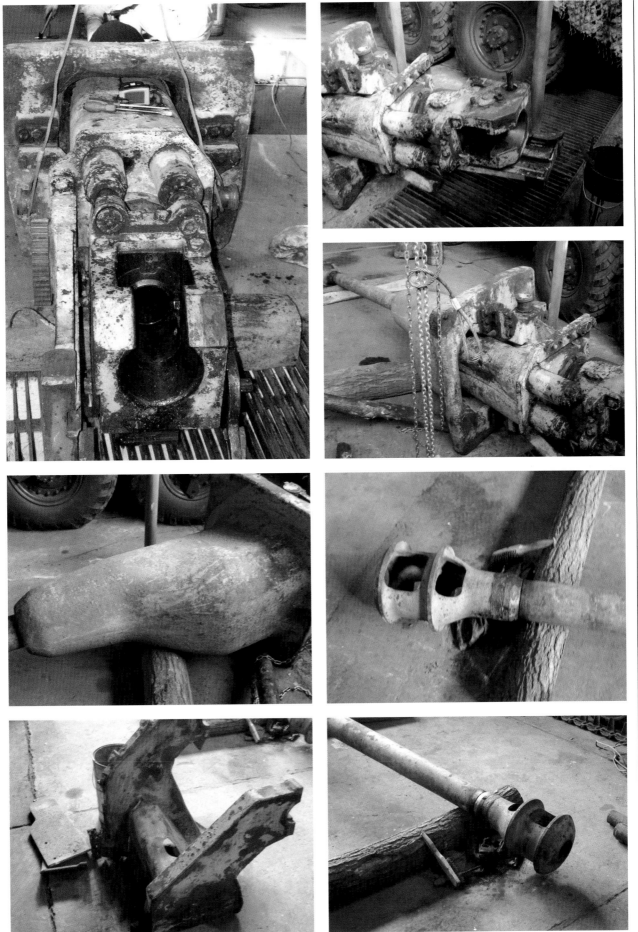

7,5 cm StuK 40 L/48 gun of *Sturmgeschütz IV* from Rgilewka river after being transported to the Armoured Weapon Museum in Poznań in 2006. After more than six decades the light shade of vehicle interior colour sheme was still almost complete. [Grzegorz Okoński]

Grzegorzew *Sturmgeschütz IV* chassis after its recovering in July 2008. [Grzegorz Okoński]

Driving sprockets of *Sturmgeschütz IV* found in Rgilewka river in Poland. It represents the *Panzerkampfwagen IV 9/BW* chassis type. [Grzegorz Okoński]

in even distances, one smaller rectangular shackle and six grips attached to mudguards. Like in the previous versions of the Sturmartillerie vehicles the edges of the plates were rounded or cut obliquely in order to prevent them from being ripped apart after a contact with terrain obstacles. In the waning period of the existence of the Third Reich new, lighter type of screens was introduced – so-called *Drahtgeflechtschürzen* or *Thoma Schürzen*. They consisted of three larger sized steel grids fitted to flats.

Inside the vehicle single – wire 12 V electric system, powered by two 600 W *Bosch GTLN 600/12-1500* or Bosch *12 B105* generators was fitted. The powerplant was started by a pair of *Bosch BNG 4/24* starters and *Bosch W 225 T1* spark plugs. In case of failure there was a possibility to start the engine manually by a crank placed in a receptacle located in the rear part of the chassis. Apart from the ignition the electric power was used for illumination of the sight and control instruments, horn, gun

The Panzerkampfwagen IV chassis of Grzegorzew *Sturmgeschütz IV*. It seems being a hybrid of *9/BW* and *Ausf. J* type. [Grzegorz Okoński]

Elements of the *Sturmgeschütz IV* from Rgilewka river transmission seen from its open hatch. [Grzegorz Okoński]

The 300 hp *Maybach HL 120 TRM* engine of Grzegorzew *Sturmgeschütz IV*. [Grzegorz Okoński]

Sturmgeschütz IV from Rgilewka river rear plate with standard *Panzerkampfwagen IV Kgs 61/400/120* tracks. The elements of muffler mountings are visible too. [Grzegorz Okoński]

Grzegorzew *Sturmgeschütz IV* chassis in one of the Army Training Centre in Poznań workshop halls. Summer of 2008. [Grzegorz Okoński]

Maybach HL 120 TRM engine of *Sturmgeschütz IV* recovered from Rgilewka during the first stage of its restoration. Poznań, 2008. [Grzegorz Okoński]

trigger, fan drive, radio, Notek tail light and external lighting. The blind of the forward light had a name of supplier of the electric equipment – Bosch GmbH – stamped on the upper part.

The main armament of the *Sturmgeschütz IV* was *7,5 cm Sturmkanone 40 L/48* gun, designed by *Rheinmetall-Borsig* factory of Düsseldorf, the same as in the ultimate, long barreled version of the equivalent based on *Panzerkampfwagen III* chassis. It was fitted with a semi-automatic breech, electric trigger and manual elevation mechanism with the range of -6° to +20°.

In the horizontal plane deflection of up to 10 degrees to each side were possible. The 3,600 mm long barrel had thity-two 0.78 mm deep right turn grooves. The guns were manufactured by *Wittenauer Maschinenfabrik AG* of Berlin and *Škoda-Werken* of Czech Pilzno. The unit cost amounted to ca. 13,500 RM.

Initially considered model of the vehicle was not fitted with a support stabilizing the barrel during transit or transport. At the end of the last autumn of the war the *Heckzurrung* folding supports in the form of a crescent – shaped reinforced steel

Assembling of *Sturmgeschütz IV* from Grzegorzew (Poland) elements. [Grzegorz Okoński]

Close ups of Grzegorzew *Sturmgeschütz IV* suspension parts. [Grzegorz Okoński]

plate placed on a threaded rod. This element was placed in a mount on a bolt hinge, and the whole assembly was fitted with an angle bar in the middle of the forward chassis section. The supported gun was angled at 6 degrees.

The ammunition reserve for the main armament amounted to 63 rounds in most vehicles. With the adaptation of the *Panzerkampfwagen IV Ausf. J* tank chassis this number rose to 87. By regulation the half were to be armor – piercing *7,5 cm Panzergranatpatrone 39* shells weighing 6.8 kg, with the muzzle velocity of 790 m/s. They enabled destroying vehicles fitted with 75 mm armor at the distance of 1,500 m or 143 mm armor at the distance of 100 m (both values concern plates angled at 30 degrees). Another type was sub-caliber *7,5 cm Panzergranatpatrone 40* (weight 4.10 kg), which thanks to the muzzle velocity of 1,060 m/s was capable of piercing a 77-mm thick plate from a distance of 1.5 km. Moreover *7,5 cm Panzergranatpatrone 38 Hochladung* shaped charge shells in three variants – A, B and C (weight 4.80 kg, muzzle velocity 485 m/s), high explosive – *7,5*

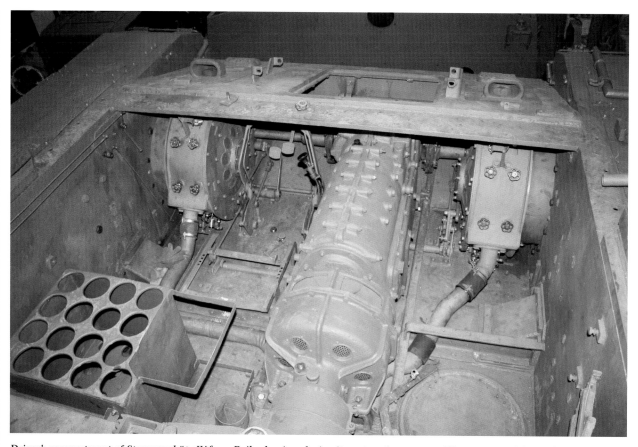

Driver's compartment of *Sturmgeschütz IV* from Rgilewka river during its restoration process. 75 mm ammunition racks are visible on the left. [Grzegorz Okoński]

cm Sprenggranatpatrone 34 (5,74 kg, 590 m/s) and smoke *7,5 cm Nebelgranatpatrone* (6,21 kg, 580 m/s) were used .

Additionally the crew had *7,92 mm Maschinengewehr 34* machine gun or later – *7,92 mm Maschinengewehr 42*. Initially the ammunition reserve was 600 rounds, but with the conversion to *Panzerkampfwagen IV Ausf. J* chassis it was increased to 2,650 rounds. The additional armament was mounted in an opening of a folding fairing in front of loader's hatch. In March 1944 rearming with *Rundumsfeuer* remote controlled units began. Often this exchange ended with the removal of this kind of weapon – in these cases the gun mount was faired over with a rectangular steel plate.

A small number of vehicles was fitted with a rotary launcher of smoke and fragmentation grenades and flares - *9,2 cm Nahverteidigungswaffe*, consisting of a barrel angled at 39° and

breech mounted on a hinge with the firing mechanism in form of a lever. Vehicles armed with this weapon were distinguished by a characteristic steel collar around the outer side of the outlet on the top of the superstructure.

At last the crew could fire personal weapons – sidearms and *9 mm Maschinenpistole 40* machine pistols. In this case the ammunition reserve amounted to 384 rounds.

Like the *Sturmgeschütz III Ausf. G* the new type of assault gun was fitted with a set of *Sfl ZF-1a/RbLF 32* sights made by *Carl Zeiss Jena*. The first was scaled from 0 to 2,300 m and the other one – from 0 to 1,400 m. In the course of time its modification *Sfl ZF-1a/RbLF 36* was introduced with even scale from 0 to 2,000 m. Both versions had 5x magnification and angle of view of 8°. Additional optical equipment comprised two driver's periscopes, from November 1944 fitted with rain covers (the

Main armament base, suspension return rollers and other elements of *Sturmgeschütz IV* found in Grzegorzew (Poland) in 2008. [Amoured Weapon Museum in Poznań (AWMP)]

Sturmgeschütz IV and *Panzerkampfwagen IV* 470x75x660 road wheels with rubber bandages. [Grzegorz Okoński]

blind spot was about six meters ahead of the front of the chassis), seven movable, circularly mounted periscopes and artillery scissor binoculars *Scherenfehrnrohr 14z mit Gitterplatte* of the commander. The vehicles armed with the remote controlled machine gun were also fitted with a 3x8 sight.

The radio communication system of the *Sturmgeschütz IV* comprised *Funkgerätsatz 15 EU* VHF receiver and 10 W *Funkgerätsatz 16 SE 10 U* transmitter. Aft of the superstructure two 2 meter long rod antennas were symmetrically installed in two stiff mounts made of hardened rubber. This suite enabled voice transmission over a distance of up to 2 km and telegraphic transmission – up to 4 km. The *Bordersprechanlage 24* intercom enabled communication among crewmembers.

The assault gun based on *Panzerkampfwagen IV* chassis was also equipped with a set of additional tools carried outside. On the left mudguard, just aft of the front light a fire extinguisher was mounted in buckles. Farther two alternately mounted wrenches were located and a small crowbar, mounted in parallel. In the rear part wire – cutting scissors and a larger crowbar were mounted.

On the other side, from front to rear the starter crank, axe, jack, track hook, pair of tow hooks and a large wrench was mounted. The shovel was mounted on the right armour plate of the engine compartment and dismantled ramrod was mounted on the other side.

The combat weight of the describer vehicle of the Sturmartillerie amounted to up to 25,900 kg. The vehicle's empty weight was 23 tonnes.

The crew of the *Sturmgeschütz IV* comprised four men. The most forward position was occupied by the driver, who had a seat with adjustable height, locked by a screw. On the left side of the combat compartment were positions of the gunner and commander, in line with the *Kommandantenkuppel* hatch. Usually the main type of uniform was gray green uniform of self-propelled artillery units, used from 1940.

Combat use

The rules of use of the *Sturmgeschütz IV* did not significantly differ from other types of German long-barrelled assault guns. Reports of losses made by individual units, in which till July 1944 there is no distinction between individual variants, seem to confirm it. As Hilary Doyle suggests the *Sonderkraftfahrzeug*

The manual ignition hatch of *Maybach HL 120 TRM* engine – the powerplant of *Sturmgeschütz IV*. [AWMP]

External view of the driver's compartment of Grzegorzew *Sturmgeschütz IV* after final restoration of vehicle's superstructure. Poznań, September 2009. The original markings of this vehicle were restored too. [Grzegorz Okoński]

Muzzle brake of 75 mm gun barrel of *Sturmgeschütz IV* from Rgilewka river. [Grzegorz Okoński]

167 term was used probably for the first time in inventory list of 15 November 1944.

A more noteworthy doctrinal element is the assignment of these vehicles to tank destroyer companies in infantry divisions, what, as it appears from tables preserved in the *Militärarchiv* of Freiburg, was a common practice. Although it was originally envisaged that each *Panzerjäger Kompanie* would have fourteen vehicles, this number was reduced to

ten in March 1944. From January 1945 the *Sturmgeschütz IVs* were also delivered to selected armour and armoured grenadier units (with the exclusion of units fighting in Italy, where these vehicles were delivered nearly a year earlier) in numbers ranging from twelve to twenty one in each. Moreover, the new vehicles entered inventories of assault gun squadrons of some large *Waffen-SS* units. Although there should have been 42 vehicles in each, the requirement was met only by the *4. SS-Polizei Panzer-Grenadier Division,* stationed at the moment of assignment in the Balkan Peninsula.

The first assault guns based on *Panzerkampfwagen IV* chassis were delivered to the 90th Armoured Grenadier Division stationed in Italy and *SS-Panzer-Abteilung 17* of the SS 17th Armoured Grenadier Division *Götz von Berlichingen.* This fact denies the information published by David Fleming that the first *Waffen-SS* unit to receive this type of vehicle the 12th SS Armoured Division *Hitlerjugend.* Interesting is that in the case of the first aforementioned units the *Sturmgeschütz IVs* replaced all previously operated tanks, which were allocated to other units operating in the Apennine Peninsula. In the same theatre of operations the *Sonderkraftfahrzeug 167s* were also assigned to 29th Armoured Grenadier Division.

In March of 1944 these vehicles debuted in tank destroyer companies of the 14th, 23rd., 32nd., 68th. and 93rd Infantry Divisions. Besides it was ordered to deliver 64 units to the SS 4th Armoured Grenadier Division *Polizei.* It was however to exclude 22 of them and assign them to the SS 5th Armoured Division *Wiking.* Further distribution was carried out in conjunction with the completion of subsequent production batches. In September of 1944 six vehicles were allocated to *Panzerlehrgang Mielau* conducting training courses on the firing range at Grafenwöhr in Bavaria. Probably it was the only organized assignment of the new version of assault gun to a training unit.

The *Saukopfsblende* gun mantlet and driving wheel with track links of Grzegorzew *Sturmgeschütz IV* during its exhibition in the Armoured Weapon Museum in Poznań, 2009. [Grzegorz Okoński]

Table 2. *Sturmgeschütz IV* (9/BW chassis) – technical data	
Dimensions	-
Length	6,700 mm
Width	2,950 mm
Height (without crane)	2,180 mm
Gun barrel muzzle elevation	1,570 mm
Combat weight	25,900 kg
Armour thickness	10– 80 mm
Engine power	300 hp
Fuel capacity	430 l
Fuel consumption	195 l/100 km
Range	-
Road	210 km
Terrain	130 km
Maximum speed	-
Road	38 km/h
Terrain	20 km/h
Armament	-
Main	7,5 cm StuK 40 L/48
Secondary	1 x 7,92 mm MG34
Ammunition reserve	-
Main armament	63 rounds
Secondary armament	600 rounds
Communication	FuG 15/FuG 16 radio set
Crew	4 men

Although most of the production output was absorbed by the demand of the infantry units some of the vehicles were also assigned to assault gun brigades. The *Sturmgeschütz Brigade 311*, fighting at Tarnopol was the first to receive them in the spring of 1944. A single example survived until the unit's surrender in Wrocław. During the next to last year of the existance of the Third Reich the guns were delivered to further ten brigades fighting on the Eastern Front as well as the *Sturmgeschütz Brigade 394* in France (this unit was smashed at Falaise, but managed to destroy 26 enemy tanks before) and *Sturmgeschütz Brigade 914* based in the Apennine Peninsula.

Like the *Sturmgeschütz III Ausf. G* the described vehicles were sent to various units as replacements – they were to substitute classic tanks. This way they got to the only large armoured unit of the Luftwaffe - *Panzer Division Hermann Göring*, or ephemeral *Führer-Begleit Brigade*.

Some captured units were used by the Red Army, among others within the 366th Guards Heavy Self-propelled Artillery Regiment, fighting in Hungary.

The Sturmgeschütz IV today

Only two units of the described assault gun have survived until present and are preserved in museum collections. Both can be admired in Poland.

The first one, currently on open-air exhibition of the Museum of White Eagle in Skarżysko-Kamienna was recovered from a swamp near Komierowo (Kuyavian-Pomeranian Voivodeship) in 1999. It belonged to middle production batch and was operated by *Stumgeschütz Brigade 276*. It was put out of action on 7 February 1945. After the crew had abandoned it the vehicle was destroyed by two 88-mm shells. Although the vehicle is incomplete, the chassis with superstructure, barrel and characteristic *Saukopfsblende* gun mount have survived in good condition. The vehicle undoubtedly requires careful preserving measures, especially due to weather factors.

The unique object is the *Sonderkraftahrzeug 167* found in 2006 by the members of the Historic&Exploration Section of the Friends of Sopot Society and enthusiasts gathered around the Field Crown Stefan Czarniecki Armoured Weapon Museum of the Army Training Centre in Poznań. For more than six decades it rested on the bottom of the Rgilewka river at Grzegorzew near Koło (Wielkopolska voivedeship). The first attempts of recovering it were made by the Polish Army in the 1950s – two T-34 medium tanks managed only to tear apart the superstructure fitted with screws. After the final recovery of all elements the vehicle has undergone major restoration at the Military Automotive Works of Poznań. It was also put into operation. It is noteworthy that the exhibit, of which the Armoured Weapon Museum has taken care, is a hybrid of the *9/BW* chassis with the *Panzerkampfwagen IV Ausf. ,J.* medium tank exhaust system. It also has a complete set of sapper's equipment and remote controlled *7,92 mm Maschinengewehr 34* machine gun assembly. Additional curiosities are the lack of frames for protective screen fitting and a trace of concrete reinforcement of commander's radome.

Despite relatively large number of the units built, the *Sturmgeschütz IV* remains overshadowed by its counterparts based on *Panzerkampfwagen III* chassis. The design, the introduction of which was indirectly initiated by the enemies of the Third Reich, like many other designs intended for the Panzerwaffe it was not able to to change the situation of the Nazi state. Nevertheless from technical point of view it belongs to most interesting types of combat vehicles and until present arouses great interest of arms history enthusiasts.

The *Saukopfsblende* gun mantlet and driving wheel with track links of Grzegorzew *Sturmgeschütz IV* during its exhibition in the Armoured Weapon Museum in Poznań, 2009. [Grzegorz Okoński]

The recovery of the Sturmgeschütz from the river Rgilewka

It was known that a StuG IV, probably of the 2. Pz.Jg.Abt. „Brandenburg" had been fleeing frim Soviet tanks. The unit was taken by surprise by them and suffered heavy losses. When the StuG rolled onto ice on the river Rgilewka the ice broke and the vehicle plummeted into water. Two German soldiers managed to escape and tried to dry themselves in Grzegorzewo. It is not known whether they were the crewmembers or desant riding on top. Some of the crewmembers, at least the driver, were killed on their positions. In the 1950s attempts to recover the vehicle were made with the use of two T-34 tanks and a railway crane. However, without avail; these efforts inflicted severe damage to the construction.

Only a wheel

During the last days of August 2006 work on the recovery of the StuG began again in Grzegorzewo. They were conducted in awful conditions – heavy rain, powerful stream of the river not yielding despite running pumps, many incidental observers and trains rolling over the bridge above the heads of people struggling with water – and ended with only a minor success. The vehicle was located quite accurately, the diver walked on it reporting what was he roughly sensing (it aroused great emotions), but a few minutes after 21.00 hours the water broke the dams and flooded the site prepared with such difficulty. Two WZT tracked recovery vehicles and excavator had to leave and instead of the StuG only its spare wheel, probably taken out of the vehicle's armour by excavator's bucket was brought to the Armoured Weapon Museum of the Army Training Centre .

Elements of Grzegorzew *Sturmgeschütz IV* interior as seen in 2009. [Grzegorz Okoński]

Elements of *Sturmgeschütz IV* from Rgilewka river in the course of their restoration, September 2009. [Jacek Szafrański]

Grzegorzew *Sturmgeschütz IV* suspension parts during their restoration. Elements of transmission, drive sprockets and springs are clearly visible. [Jacek Szafrański]

They did not give up

The second action was carried out a month later and instead of several leaders Captain Tomasz Ogrodniczuk, the curator of the Armoured Weapon Museum was in command. He described this event in the following words: "the vehicle was probably trying to make to the other side under the bridge and is positioned with the gun toward the bridge. The recovery team began to dig the vehicle out from the bank (towards Warsaw), willing to reach the side of the StuG that way. As it turned out later, this

Grzegorzew *Sturmgeschütz IV* transmission elements photographed in the course of their restoration in 2009. [Grzegorz Okoński]

pricked element was a blown up buttress of the bridge. This mistake cost us the loss of possibility to dig in depth, because the excavator could not close to the scarp, which was constantly sliding. Shovels, firehose and a mine pump were put in motion. At the end of the day metal parts and ripped out elements of sheet metal and armour plates appeared. Quick dusk held back the operation and the lines had not been attached yet. On 30 September the operation was resumed after 5 a.m. (...) Dam and recovery teams were doing their best to attach the lines to the vehicle's hooks. Then work on positioning two WZT-2 recovery vehicles and attaching the lines to winches began. During recovery attempt both hooks break, there can be only one decision: another pumping out the water and burning out four openings for two lines in the superstructure with the torch. After the openings had been made and lines had been attached the vehicle began to surface. Outlines of the superstructure and gun were visible but the hull was still stuck in mud". The hull, wheels and tracks remained in the Rgilewka.

The numbers emerge

The superstructure with the gun and many smaller elements recovered from the river were transported to Poznań and there at the museum they were washed under pressure. The primer paint, white crosses and numbers 981 and 968 were revealed. They were probably painted during the assembly to mark individual elements. Moreover, the number 88361 stamped in the armor was revealed on parts of the hull. During this work it turned out that the armoured monument is a peculiar hybrid – it was built on the basis of parts of the StuG III, the earlier type of the self-propelled gun.

The last phase of recovery of the remaining parts of the vehicle – the "tub" with chassis took place in July of 2008. Inside the vehicle about 50 rounds of ammunition, weapons and equipment of the crew were found. The rebuilt StuG IV is now an exhibit of the Armoured Weapons Museum in Poznań.

Bibliography

Source materials

Militärarchiv Freiburg, Signature: RH 10/349-350, *Zuweisungen von Panzern, Sturmgeschützen etc.*

Militärarchiv Freiburg, Signature: RH 10/106, *Übersicht der von Aug 1943 - Apr 45 in Umgliederung und Auffrischung befindlichen Panzerjäger-Abt.*

Table 3. *Sturmgeschütz IV* in the independent Sturmgeschütz brigades.

Area of operations	Unit
Eastern front	Sturmgeschütz Brigade 226
	Sturmgeschütz Brigade 236
	Sturmgeschütz Brigade 239
	Sturmgeschütz Brigade 259
	Sturmgeschütz Brigade 276
	Sturmgeschütz Brigade 277
	Sturmgeschütz Brigade 279
	Sturmgeschütz Brigade 311
	Sturmgeschütz Brigade 904
	Sturmgeschütz Brigade 912
	Sturmgeschütz Lehrbrigade II
Western front	Sturmgeschütz Brigade 394
Italian front	Sturmgeschütz Brigade 914

Militärarchiv Freiburg, Signature: RH 10/352, *Panzer-, StuG-, Pak-Sf.-, gp.Kfz.-Lage 30.12.44/15.1.45.*

Literature

Chamberlain Peter, *Encyclopedia of German Tanks of World War Two*, Phoenix 1999.

De Sisto Frank, *German Sturmartillerie at War vol. 1*, Hong Kong 2008.

De Sisto Frank, *German Sturmartillerie at War vol. 2*, Hong Kong 2009.

Doyle Hilary, *Sturmgeschütz III & IV 1942-1945*, Oksford 2001.

Fleischer Wolfgang, *Deutsche Sturmgeschütze im Einsatz*, Wölfersheim-Berstadt 1999.

Fleming David, *Weapons of the Waffen SS*, St Paul 2003.

Gładysiak Łukasz, *Niemieckie długolufowe działa szturmowe. Sturmgeschütz III Ausf. F – F/8 – G*, [w:] „Militaria XX wieku. Wydanie Specjalne Nr 16", Lublin 2010.

Jentz Thomas, *Panzertruppen. The Complete Guide to the Creation & Combat Empolyment of Germany's Tank Force 1943-1945*, Atglen 1996.

Jentz Thomas, *Sturmgeschuetz. S.Pak to Sturmmoerser*, Darlington 1999.

Koch Fred, *Funkgeräte in Gepanzerten Fahrzeugen der Wehrmacht*, Wölfersheim-Berstadt 1999.

Koch Fred, *Laufwerke und Ketten deutscher Panzerkampfwagen 1935-1945*, Wölfersheim-Berstadt 1998.

Perrett Bryan, *Sturmartillerie & Panzerjäger*, Oxford 1999.

Trojca Waldemar, *Sd.Kfz. 161 Pz.Kpfw. IV Ausf. G/H/J vol. 2*, Katowice 2005.

Table 4. *Sturmgeschütz IV* deployment – infantry divisions and *Volksgrenadier* divisions, march-december 1944

	Unit	Amount of vehicles	Area of operations		Unit	Amount of vehicles	Area of operations
March 1944	14. Infanterie Division	10	Eastern front	July 1944	126. Infanterie Division	10	Eastern front
	32. Infanterie Division	10	Eastern front		197. Infanterie Division	10	Eastern front
	68. Infanterie Division	10	Eastern front		253. Infanterie Division	10	Eastern front
	93. Infanterie Division	10	Eastern front		290. Infanterie Division	14	Eastern front
	129. Infanterie Division	10	Eastern front		299. Infanterie Division	14	Eastern front
	Monthly amount:	50	-		Monthly amount:	95	-
April 1944	23. Infanterie Division	10	Eastern front	August 1944	96. Infanterie Division	10	Eastern front
	26. Infanterie Division	10	Eastern front		121. Infanterie Division	10	Eastern front
	31. Infanterie Division	10	Eastern front		254. Infanterie Division	10	Eastern front
	36. Infanterie Division	10	Eastern front		292. Infanterie Division	10	Eastern front
	57. Infanterie Division	10	Eastern front		329. Infanterie Division	10	Eastern front
	81. Infanterie Division	10	Eastern front		Monthly amount:	50	-
	88. Infanterie Division	10	Eastern front	September 1944	34. Infanterie Division	10	Italian front
	134. Infanterie Division	10	Eastern front		211. Infanterie Division	10	Eastern front
	331. Infanterie Division	10	Germany		340. Infanterie Division	10	Eastern front
	389. Infanterie Division	10	Eastern front		361. Infanterie Division	10	Eastern front
	Monthly amount:	100	-		Monthly amount:	40	-
May 1944	12. Infanterie Division	10	Eastern front	October 1944 r.	24. Infanterie Division	10	Eastern front
	30. Infanterie Division	10	Eastern front		36. Infanterie Division	10	Eastern front
	35. Infanterie Division	10	Eastern front		83. Infanterie Division	10	Eastern front
	45. Infanterie Division	10	Eastern front		100. Jäger Division	10	Eastern front
	95. Infanterie Division	10	Eastern front		102. Infanterie Division	10	Eastern front
	110. Infanterie Division	10	Eastern front		205. Infanterie Division	10	Eastern front
	131. Infanterie Division	10	Eastern front		389. Infanterie Division	10	Eastern front
	206. Infanterie Division	10	Eastern front		Monthly amount:	70	-
	267. Infanterie Division	10	Eastern front	November 1944	89. Infanterie Division	10	Western front
	342. Infanterie Division	10	Eastern front		348. Infanterie Division	10	Western front
	Monthly amount:	100	-		353. Infanterie Division	10	Western front
June 1944	11. Infanterie Division	10	Eastern front		Monthly amount:	30	-
	58. Infanterie Division	10	Eastern front	December 1944	11. Infanterie Division	10	Eastern front
	61. Infanterie Division	10	Eastern front		215. Infanterie Division	10	Eastern front
	320. Infanterie Division	10	Eastern front		263. Infanterie Division	10	Eastern front
	337. Infanterie Division	10	Eastern front		12. Volksgrenadier Division	10	Western front
	Monthly amount:	50	-		19. Volksgrenadier Division	3	Western front
July 1944	1. Infanterie Division	10	Eastern front		36. Volksgrenadier Division	5	Western front
	101. Infanterie Division	10	Eastern front		353. Volksgrenadier-Division	10	Western front
	121. Infanterie Division	10	Eastern front		Monthly amount:	58	-
	122. Infanterie Division	7	Eastern front				

Table 5. *Sturmgeschütz IV* deployment – armoured divisions and Panzergrenadier divisions, 1945

	Unit	Amount of vehicles	Area of operations
January 1945	4. Panzer Division	14	Eastern Front
	20. Panzer Division	10	Eastern front
	Pz.Gr.Div. *Brandenburg*	21	Eastern front
	Monthly amount:	45	-
February 1945	10. Panzer Grenadier Division	12	Eastern front
	Führer Grenadier Division	21	Eastern front
	Monthly amount:	33	-
March 1945	2. Panzer Division	10	Western front
	Monthly amount:	10	-

Table 6. *Sturmgeschütz IV* deployment – Waffen-SS divisions, first half of 1944

	Unit	Amount of vehicles	Area of operations
February 1944	17. SS Pz.Gr. Division	5	Western front
	Mounthly amount:	5	-
March 1944	4. SS-Polizei Pz.Gr. Division	42	Italian front
	5. SS Panzer Division	22	Eastern front
	17. SS Pz.Gr. Division	20	Western front
	Monthly amount:	84	-
April 1944	17. SS Pz.Gr. Division	17	Western front
	Monthly amount:	17	-

Table 7. *Sturmgeschütz IV* deployment as the reinforcement weapon

	Unit	Area of operations
Wehrmacht	1. Panzer Division	Eastern front
	Panzer Division *Feldherrnhalle*	Eastern front
	Führer Begleit Brigade	Eastern front
Luftwaffe	Fl-Pz. Division *Hermann Göring*	Eastern front
Waffen-SS	1. SS Panzer Division	Western front
	2. SS Panzer Division	Western front
	3. SS Panzer Division	Western front
	10. SS Panzer Division	Western front
	12. SS Panzer Division	Western front
	18. SS Freiw. Pz.Gr. Division	Eastern front

Front and rear view of *Sturmgeschütz IV* recovered in Grzegorzew (Poland) after its final restoration. Nowadays the vehicle is exhibited in the Armoured Weapon Museum of the Army Training Centre in Poznań. [Jacek Szafrański]

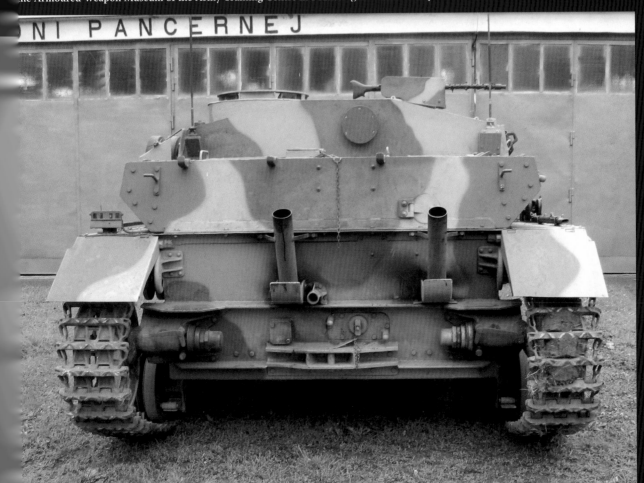

Sturmgeschütz IV exhibited in the Armoured Weapon Museum in Poznań is the one and only fully opeartive exemplar worldwide. Some times it leaves Museum being sent for example to historical-reenactement events in Wielkopolska. [Jacek Szafrański]

[Mikołaj Klorek]

Grzegorzew *Sturmgeschütz IV* was presented to the wider audience in Poznań, in 2010. That year final restoration of this vehicle had been completed. [Jacek Szafrański]

The return roller of Grzegorzew *Sturmgeschütz IV* made completely of steel is characteristic especially for *Panzerkampfwagen IV Ausf. J* medium tank. Next to this element the fuel filler flap is visible.

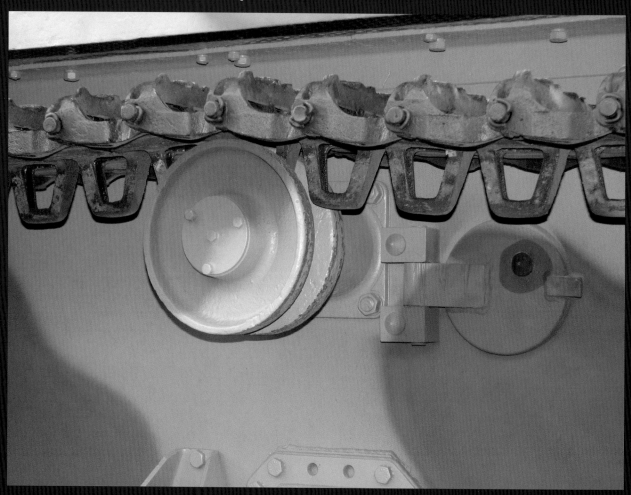

Grzegorzew *Sturmgeschütz IV* suspension cart close up with bumper and massive mounting shield. [Jacek Szafrański]

Panzerkampfwagen IV 470x75x660 road wheels with rubber bandages of *Sturmgeschütz IV* exhibited in Poznań. [Jacek Szafrański]

Grzegorzew *Sturmgeschütz IV* idler wheel with standard *Panzerkampfwagen IV* track links. [Jacek Szafrański]

The same vehicle road wheels close up. [Jacek Szafrański]

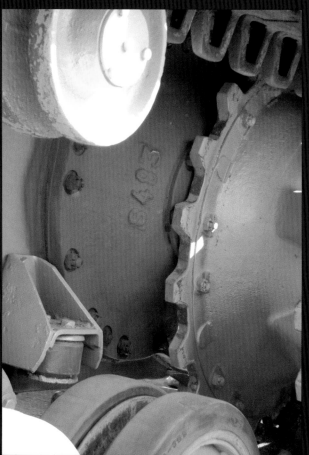

Details of the drive sprocket and suspension cart mounting shield of *Sturmgeschütz IV* from Poznań. [Jacek Szafrański]

The return roller of *Sturmgeschütz IV* recovered from Rgilewka river. [Jacek Szafrański]

Standard *Panzerkampfwagen IV* road wheels with rubber bandages installed in Grzegorzew *Sturmgeschütz IV* (on this and next two pages) [Jacek Szafrański]

Late variant of *Panzerkampfwagen IV* drive sprocket installed in *Sturmgeschütz IV* exhibited in the Museum of Armoured Weapon in Poznań.

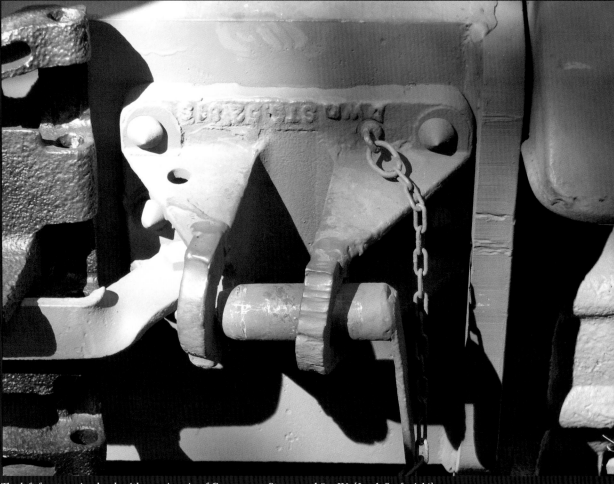

The left front towing hook with massive pin of Grzegorzew *Sturmgeschütz IV*. [Jacek Szafrański]

Sturmgeschütz IV from Rgilewka river suspension springs rear view. [Grzegorz Okoński]

The same vehicle chassis seen from below (on this and next page). [Grzegorz Okoński]

[Grzegorz Okoński]

[Grzegorz Okoński]

Grzegorzew *Sturmgeschütz IV* spare track links installed on the chassis front plates. Spare tracks were very often created an extra armour. [Jacek Szafrański]

Left front fender spring of Grzegorzew *Sturmgeschütz IV* identical to *Panzerkampfwagen IV* ones. [Jacek Szafrański]

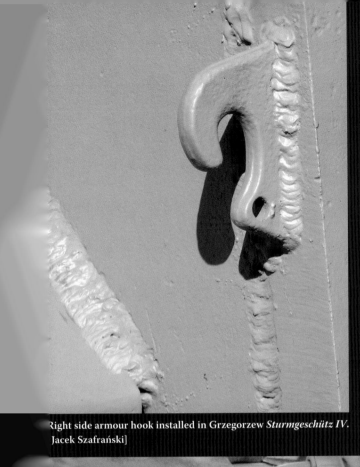

Right side armour hook installed in Grzegorzew *Sturmgeschütz IV*. [Jacek Szafrański]

Sturmgeschütz IV transmission detail seen from its opened left hatch. [Łukasz Kaźmierski]

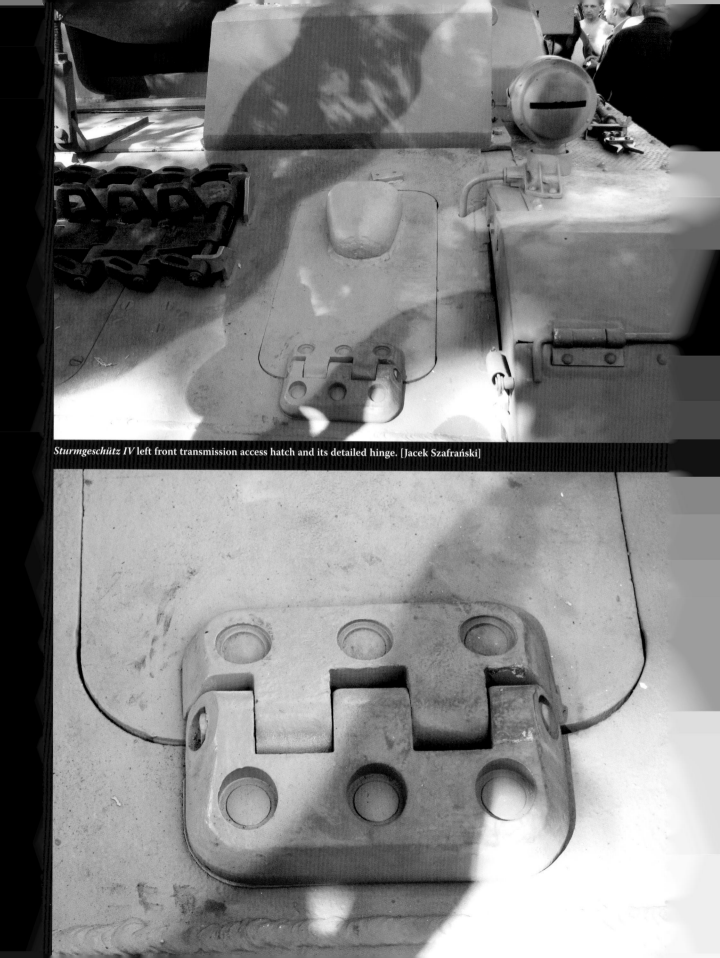

Sturmgeschütz IV left front transmission access hatch and its detailed hinge. [Jacek Szafrański]

Grzegorzew *Sturmgeschütz IV* driver compartment front armour with periscopes and their protection. [Jacek Szafrański]

Transport hitch of *StuK 40 L/48* barrel installed in *Sturmgeschütz IV* exhibited in Poznań. [Jacek Szafrański]

The element presented on page 45 seen from a different angle. [Jacek Szafrański]

Massive muzzle brake and *Saukopfsblende* gun mantlet of Grzegorzew *Sturmgeschütz IV* (on this and next page). [Jacek Szafrański]

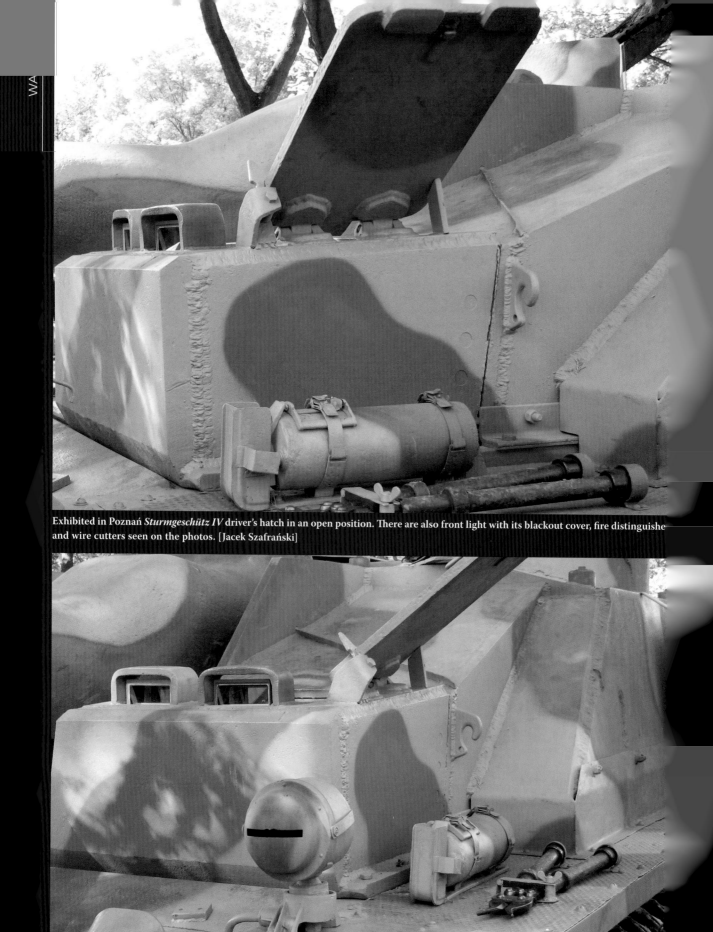

Exhibited in Poznań *Sturmgeschütz IV* driver's hatch in an open position. There are also front light with its blackout cover, fire distinguishe and wire cutters seen on the photos. [Jacek Szafrański]

Grzegorzew *Sturmgeschütz IV* front light made by *Bosch GmbH* company of Stuttgart. [Jacek Szafrański]

The same vehicle driver's compartment left wall with external stowage installed on the fender. [Jacek Szafrański]

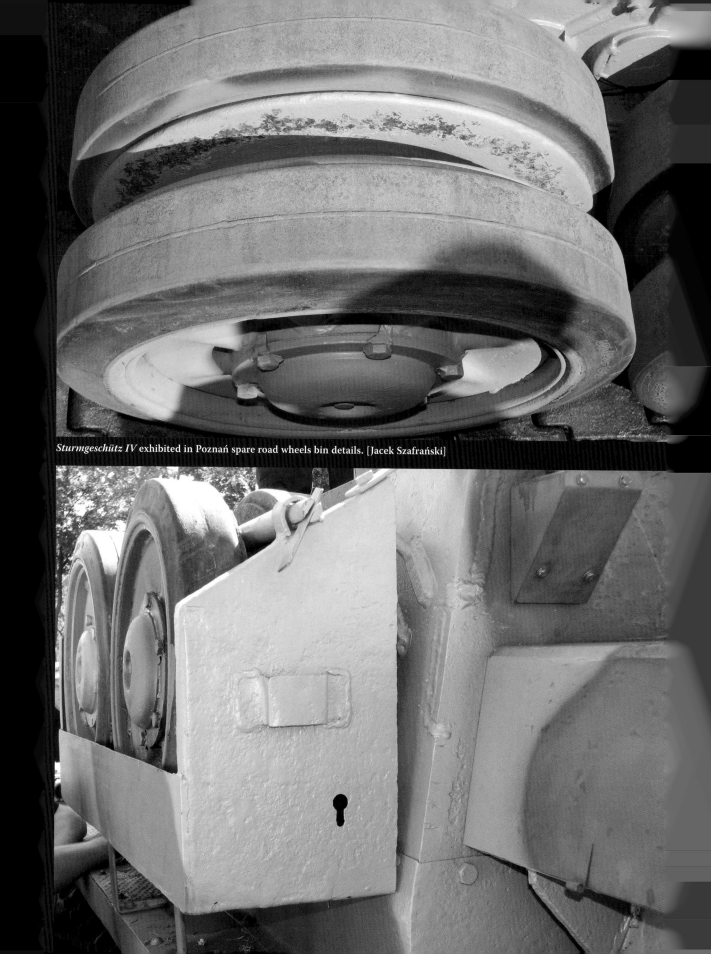

Sturmgeschütz IV exhibited in Poznań spare road wheels bin details. [Jacek Szafrański]

Grzegorzew *Sturmgeschütz IV* spare road wheels bin installed on the left wall of vehicle's hull. [Jacek Szafrański]

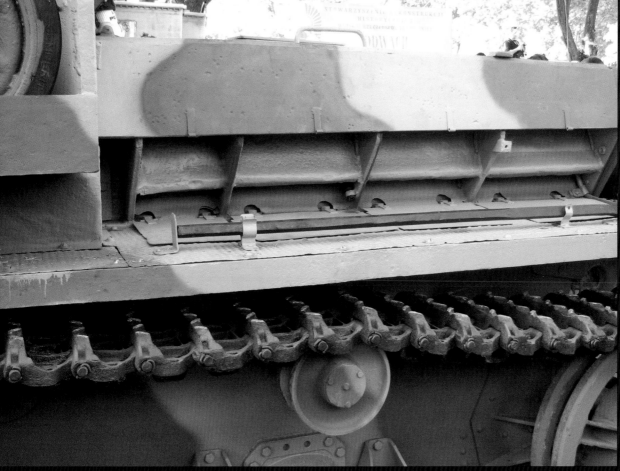

Sturmgeschütz IV exhibited in Poznań engine compartment left air intake. [Jacek Szafrański]

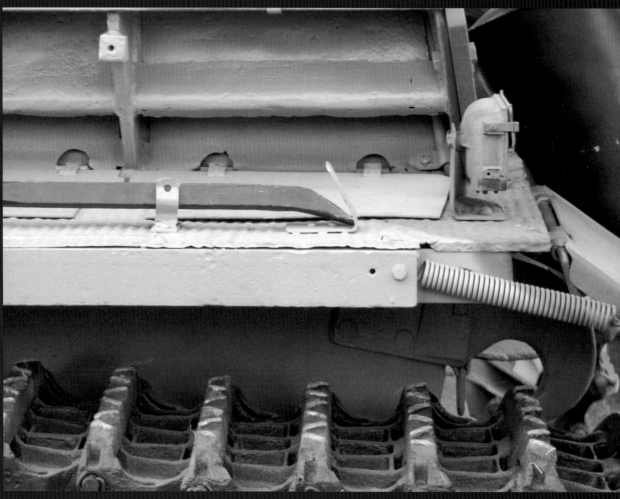

The crowbar, spring and rear *Notek* light installed in the rear part of Grzegorzew *Sturmgeschütz IV* left fender. [Jacek Szafrański]

Sturmgeschütz IV from Rgilewka river rear *Notek* light and left fender spring. [Jacek Szafrański]

Grzegorzew *Sturmgeschütz IV* track links mounted on the left idler wheel. Elements of track tension mechanism are clearly visible too. [Jacek Szafrański]

Grzegorzew *Sturmgeschütz IV* exhibited in the Museum of Armored Weapon in Poznań suspension springs rear view. [Jacek Szafrański]

Grzegorzew *Sturmgeschütz IV* rear armour plate with a late type *Panzerkampfwagen IV* mufflers. Unfortunately original mufflers did no survived. [Jacek Szafrański]

Grzegorzew *Sturmgeschütz IV* rear towing hook with an extra boot device hatch visible above. [Jacek Szafrański]

Right track tension mechanism of *Sturmgeschütz IV* from Rgilewka river. [Jacek Szafrański]

Sturmgeschütz IV from Rgilewka river late type mufflers. [Jacek Szafrański]

Rear armour plate of Grzegorzew *Sturmgeschütz IV* right corner details. [Jacek Szafrański]

The same element as on previous page seen from another angle. [Jacek Szafrański]

Sturmgeschütz IV from Rgilewka river engine compartment right air intake details (on this and next page). [Jacek Szafrański]

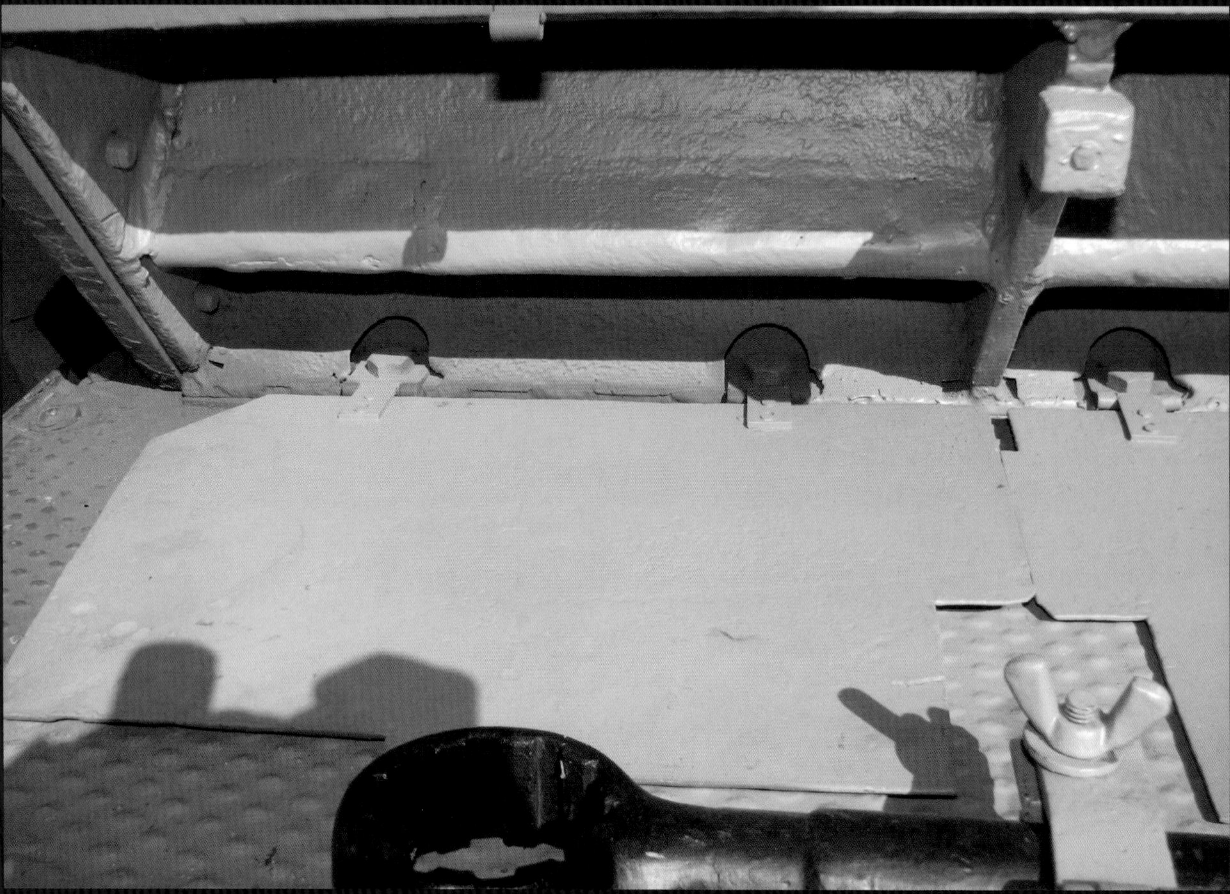

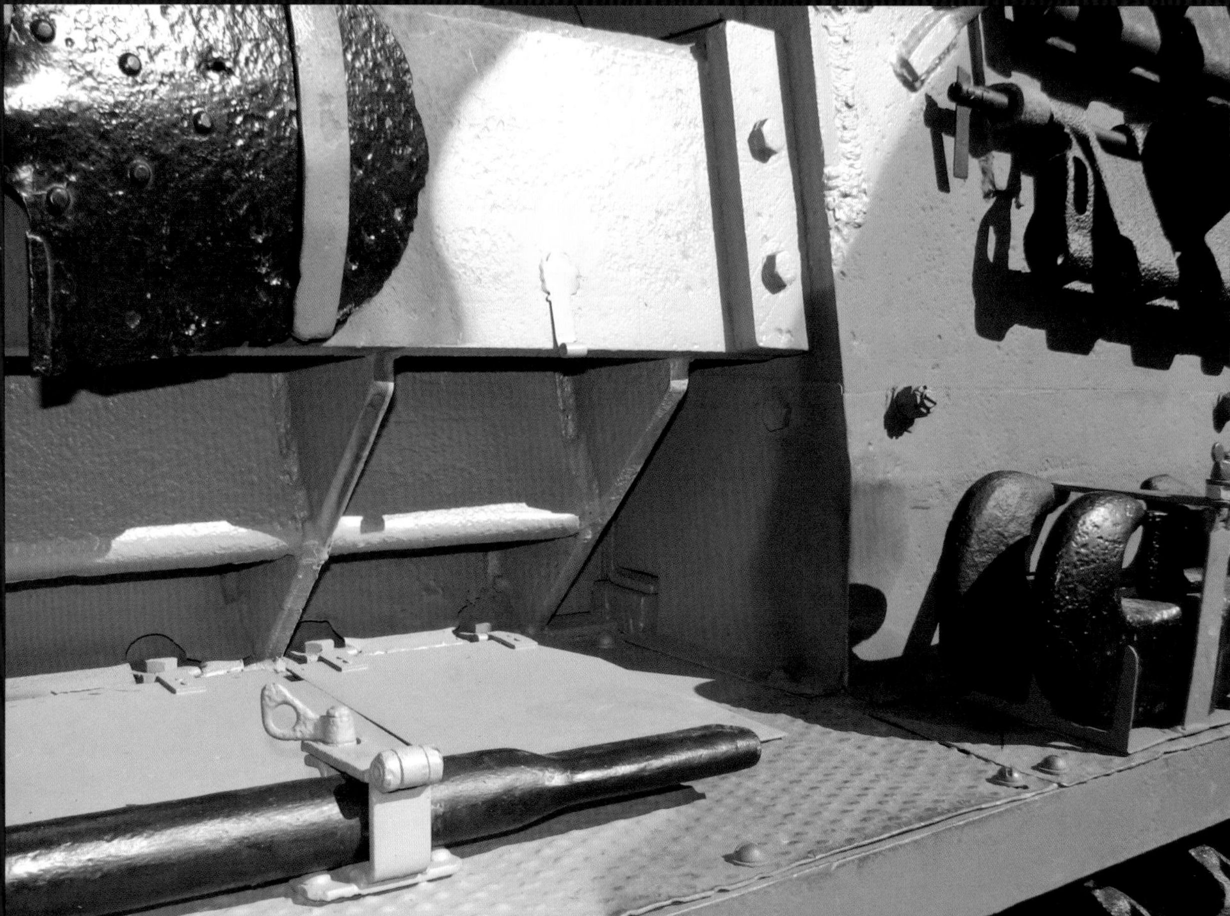

Grzegorzew *Sturmgeschütz IV* right fender seen from behind. Towing hooks, spade and track tension wrench are possible to identify. [Jacek Szafrański]

C-shaped towing hooks and spare track links of *Sturmgeschütz IV* from Rgilewka river. [Jacek Szafrański]

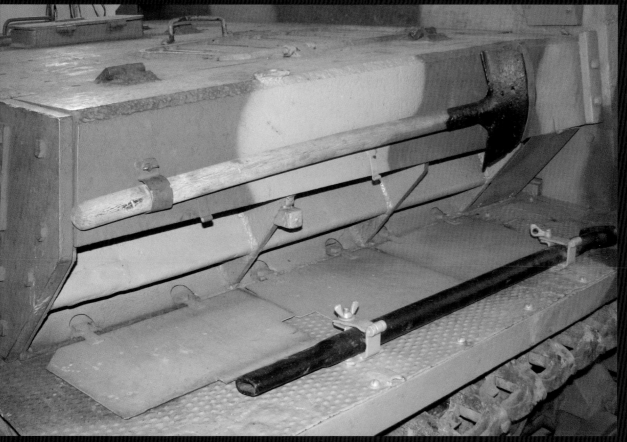

Sturmgeschütz IV from the Museum of Armoured Weapon in Poznań engine compartment right air intake with spade and track tension wrench in appropriate place. [Jacek Szafrański]

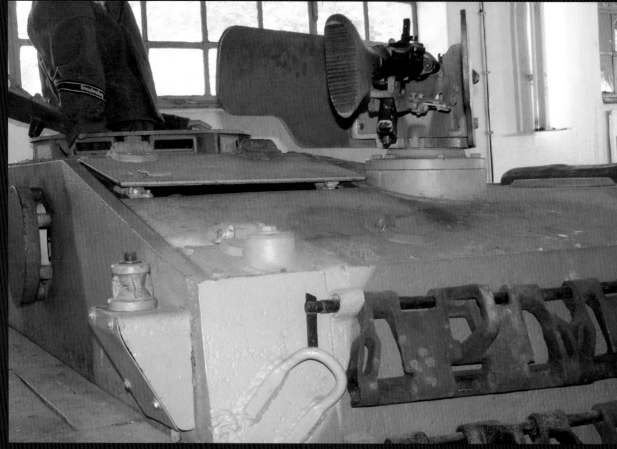

Sturmgeschütz IV loader's hatch in closed position with *Rundumsfeuer* machine gun device. [Jacek Szafrański]

Sturmgeschütz IV from Rgilewka river combat compartment hull right rear corner with antenne and 2-tonne crane sockets. [Jacek Szafrański]

Grzegorzew *Sturmgeschütz IV* antenne sockets with slots made of rubber installed on the rear wall of combat compartment hull. [Grzegorz Okoński]

Sturmgeschütz IV from Rgilewka river right antenna socket as seen from two different angles. [Jacek Szafrański]

Grzegorzew *Sturmgeschütz IV* loader's hatch in the open position. [Jacek Szafrański]

Left front part of *Sturmgeschütz IV* exhibited in Poznań seen from the commander cupola. [Jacek Szafrański]

Rundumsfeuer remote control device with *7,92 mm Maschinengewehr 34* belong to Grzegorzew *Sturmgeschütz IV*. [Jacek Szafrański]

Sturmgeschütz IV from Rgilewka river commander cupola with scissor binoculars hatch open. The rangefinder mounting location is clearly visible too. [Jacek Szafrański]

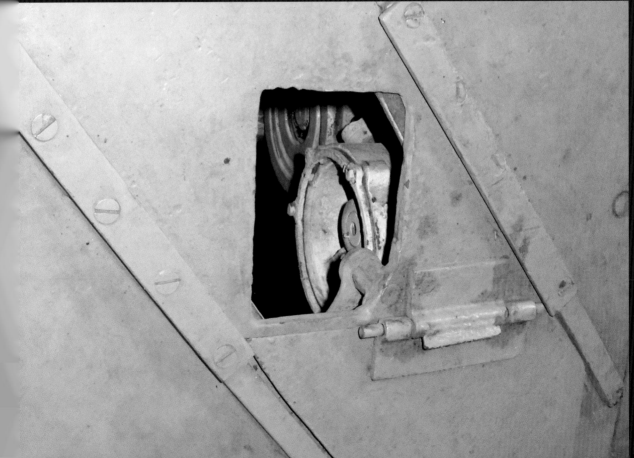

Sturmgeschütz IV from Rgilewka river commander cupola with its hatch in a closed position. [Jacek Szafrański]

Maybach HL 120 TRM engine access hatch of *Sturmgeschütz IV* from Rgilewka river. [Jacek Szafrański]

Grzegorzew *Sturmgeschütz IV* spare road wheels in bin seen from above. [Jacek Szafrański]

Sturmgeschütz IV from the Museum of Armoured Weapon in Poznań commander supola interior. [Jacek Szafrański]

The inner part of Grzegorzew *Sturmgeschütz IV* loader's position. There is the *9,2 cm Nahverteidigungswaffen* grenade launcher visible on the left. [Grzegorz Okoński]

Grzegorzew *Sturmgeschütz IV* main armament – *7,5 cm StuK 40 L/48* gun seen from combat compartment interior. [Grzegorz Okoński]

Commander's and gunner's seats of *Sturmgeschütz IV* from Rgilewka river. [Grzegorz Okoński]

Grzegorzew *Sturmgeschütz IV* gunner's position seen from the commander's seat. [Grzegorz Okoński]

The same vehicle combat compartment right rear corner close up. [Grzegorz Okoński]

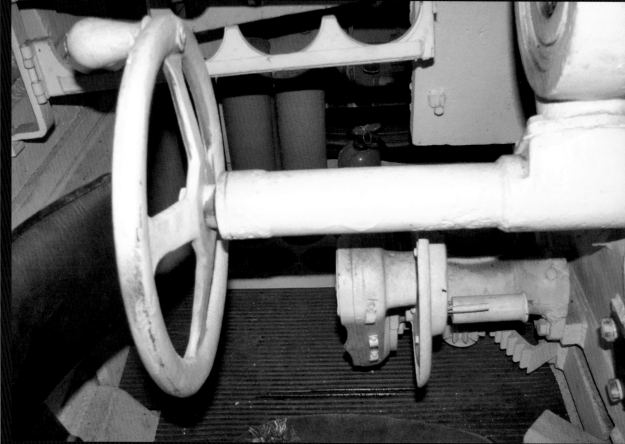

Sturmgeschütz IV main armament – *7,5 cm StuK 40 L/48* gun details (on this and next page). [Jacek Szafrański]

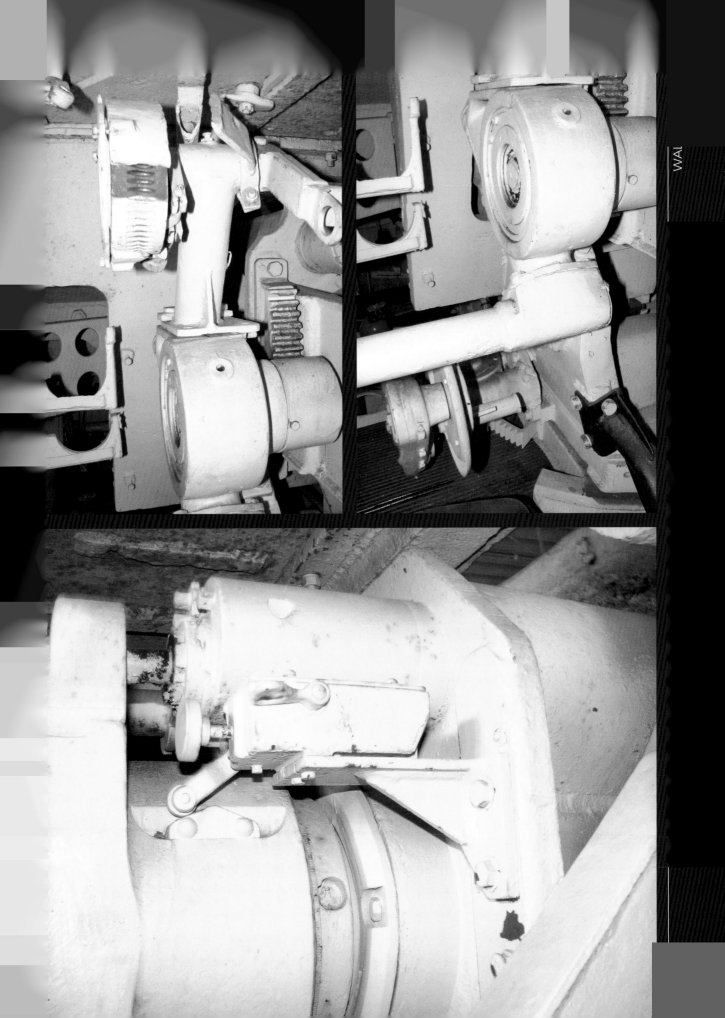

9,2 cm Nahverteidigungswaffen inner part seen from *Sturmgeschütz IV* loader's position. [Jacek Szafrański]

Exhibited in Poznań *Sturmgeschütz IV* driver's seat seen from his access hatch [Grzegorz Okoński].

The same vehicle driving levers and pedals seen from above. [Grzegorz Okoński].

Grzegorzew *Sturmgeschütz IV* driver's compartment details (on this and next page). [Grzegorz Okoński/Jacek Szafrański]

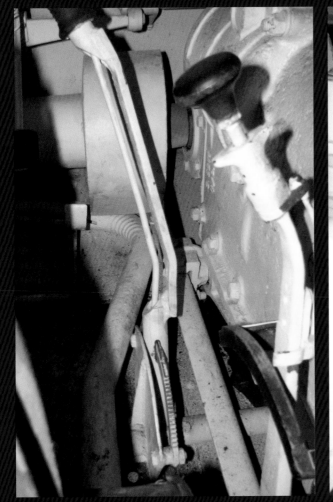

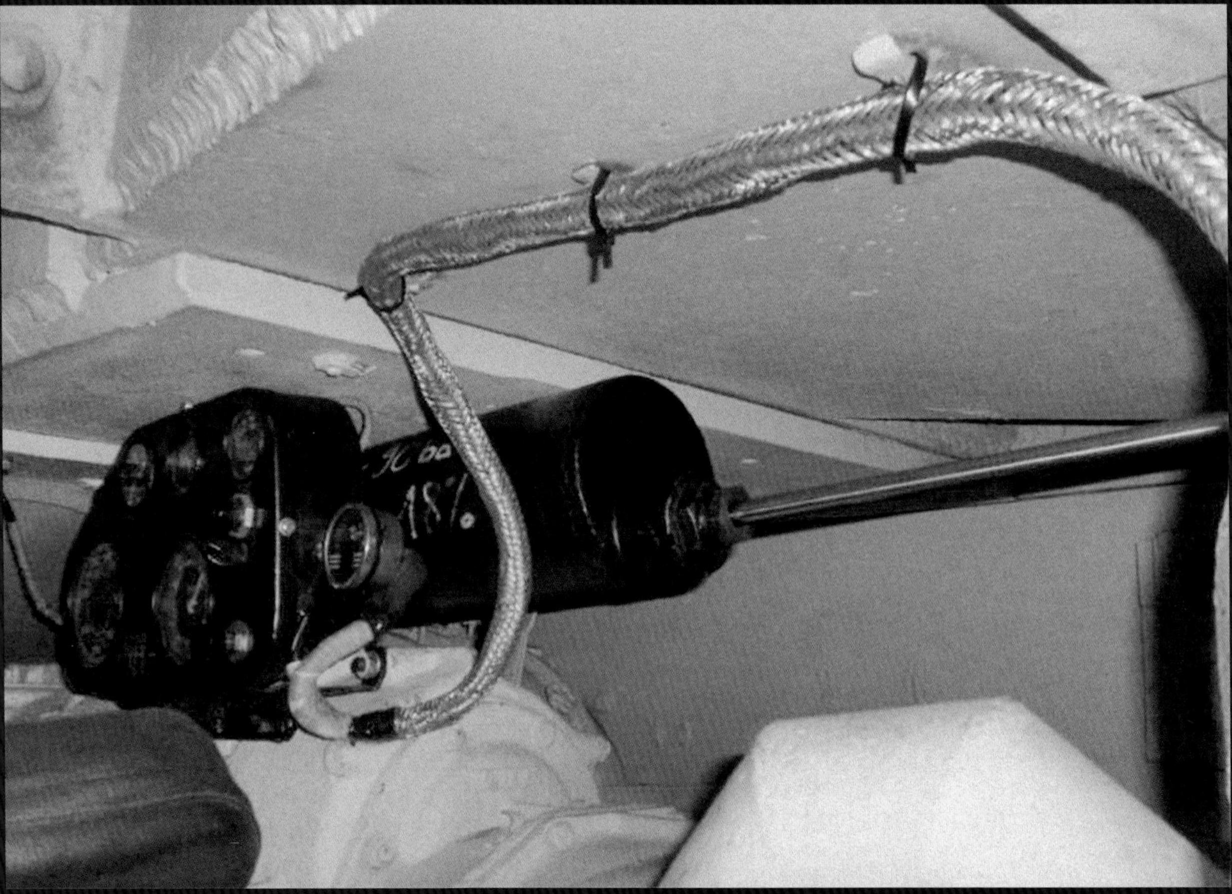

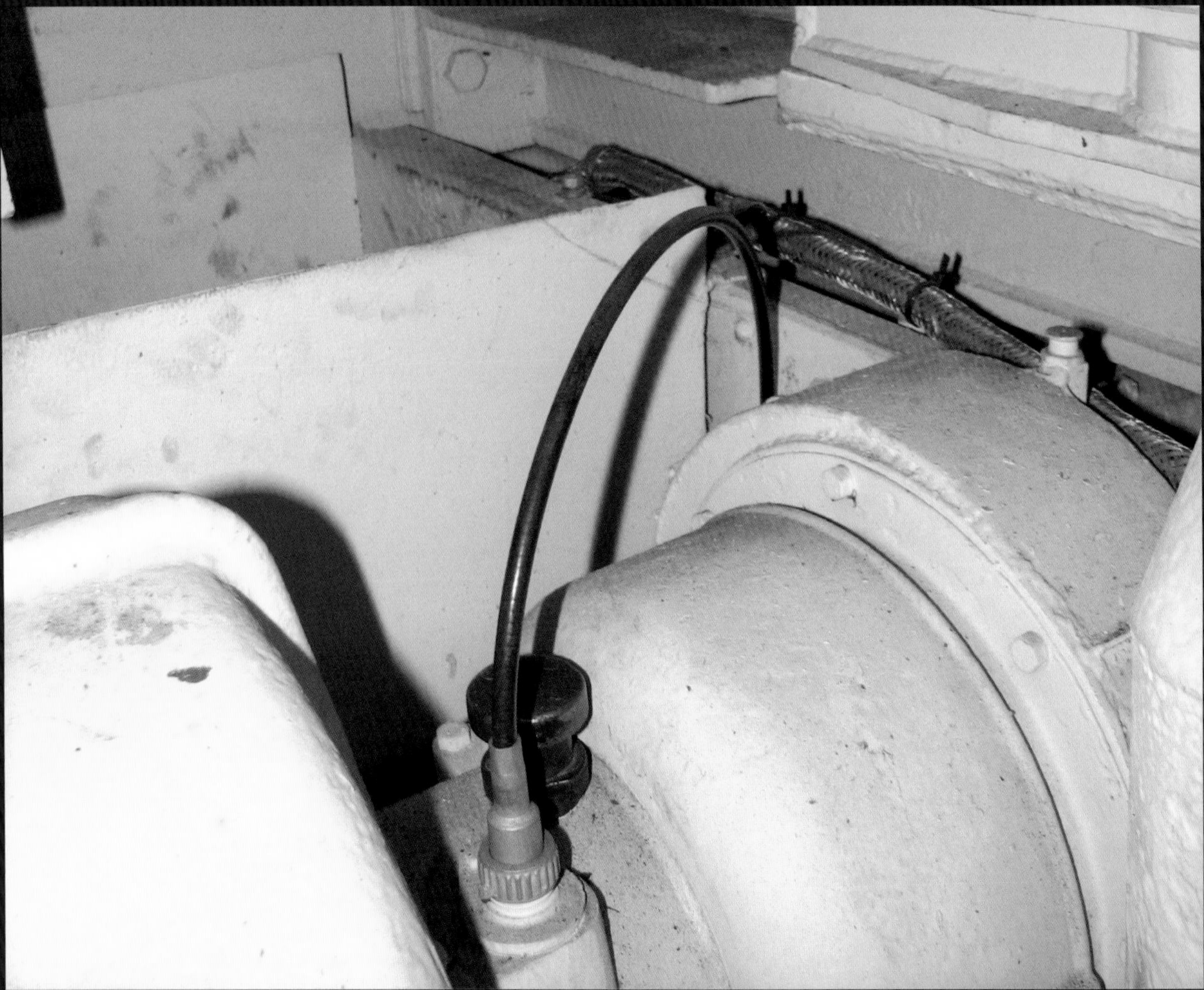

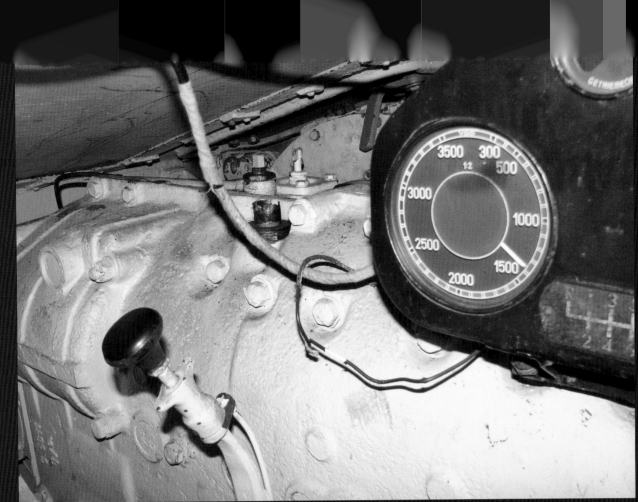

Sturmgeschütz IV from the Museum of Armoured Weapon in Poznań dashboard installed on the right side of driver's combat compartment. [Jacek Szafrański]

German self-propelled or assault artillery soldiers (vehicle crew members) photographed during the campaign in the eastern front. The *Feldgrau* special uniforms as well as forage caps are clearly visible.

The gray green (*Feldgrau*) uniforms of the German self-propelled artillery crews were widely used also by the soldiers of the *Sturmgeschütz IV* units. It usually consisted of field or forage cap made of woolen cloth and characteristic open-neck, fasten assimetrically field jacket made of the same material (or herringbone twill one especially in summer). The uniform set complemented gray green trousers designed especially for amoured units soldiers and black or brown leather laced shoes.

Field equipement of *Sturmgeschütz IV* crew members were reduced only to the leather or, mainly in the last months of World War II, webbing main belt with pistol holster for example 9 mm P.08 or Walther P.38. Other armament, such as *Maschinenpistole 40* machine pistols were installed in the special racks inside the vehicle's combat compartment.

The silhouette was prepared for and presented in "Poznań 1945. Armoured Weapon" exhibition of Museum of Armaments, Wielkopolska Museum of Independence Campaigns in Poznań. Photo by Łukasz Dyczkowski / Stowarzyszenie Niezależnych Fotoreporterów Tropiciel Historii.

Colours

Self-propelled guns were subject to the same painting rules as all other military vehicles built in the Third Reich. In practice at the moment of the beginning of the production in December of 1943 the paint schemes of vehicles and other equipment of the army was regulated by rules introduced in February of 1943. They introduced the Dunkelgelb nach Muster (later codified as RAL 7028), which had light tan – brown shade as the basic camouflage paint. Supplementing colours were Rotbraun RAL 8017 (red brown) and Olivgrün RAL 6003 (dark olive green). In practice the vehicles were covered uniformly with the basic RAL 7028 paint in the factory, supplemented with the crosses. Vehicles painted so were leaving the factory and being delivered to the units. Only in the unit the paint scheme was supplemented with RAL8017 and RAL6003 paints supplied in the form of paste. Obviously it resulted in a vast diversity of paint schemes, although some sort of consistency of the paint schemes within individual units can be noted, since the unit maintenance crews (in practice – a few men) were responsible for painting. It was a reasonable attitude, because the camouflage was adapted to local conditions, in which the vehicles operated. Moreover, thanks to proper diluting of the paints supplied as pastes lighter and darker shades of green and brown could be obtained. Usually the paint job was done with spray guns, but painting with brushes was also practised especially in winter, when white camouflage paint was applied.

The formal rules of vehicle painting were changed in August of 1944, when the tank manufacturers were ordered to apply the camouflage in the factory; over the basic RAL 7028 colour large RAL8017 and RAL6003 spots were to be applied. Subsequently in November new rules of factory painting were introduced: the basic paint was to be green RAL6003, over which sharp-contoured RAL8017 and RAL 7028 were to be applied by spraying. Interesting is that while the tank manufacturers quickly began to obey these rules, the assault gun, both StuG III and StuG IV manufacturer the Krupp-Grusson Werke AG followed only in early 1945. An example is the StuG IV recovered from the Rgilewka river, built in December of 1944, which was covered with the basic Dunkelgelb paint.

Regardless of it in the units several markings, like tactical numbers (one, two, three or even four-digit) were applied (the StuG IVs of the *4. SS-Polizei-Panzergrenadier-Division* sported such four-digit numbers) or the unit markings (badges) etc. Here the practice of individual units was in power. The StuG IV assault guns were delivered to various units, so there was a significant diversity in this field. The main operators of these vehicles were independent assault gun battalions and brigades, in which they were used along with the StuG IIIs. Other users were antitank units (Pz.Jg.Abt.), assigned both to infantry and armoured grenadier divisions and armoured divisions as well. In the latter the StuG IVs were sometimes assigned to regular armoured battalions equipped with Panzer IV tanks (e.g. SS-Panzer-Division *Wiking*).

Marek Jaszczołt

Sturmgeschütz IV, **tactical number 4301, of SS-Panzer-Abteilung 4 (*4. SS-Polizei-Panzergrenadier-Division*). Hungary, November 1944. Note the first, left Schürzen screen probably being taken from a different German armoured vehicle.**

**Painted by
Tomasz Idzikowski**

Painted by
Tomasz Idzikowski

Sturmgeschütz IV, tactical number 22,
of an unidentified German unit.
Eastern front, Summer 1944.

Painted by
Tomasz Idzikowski

Sturmgeschütz IV named *Kunigunde*, of an unidentified German unit. Western front, Spring 1945. The vehicle represents the last type of camouflage scheme applied on the Wehrmacht armoured vehicles with a dark green background instead sand yellow one.

Sturmgeschütz IV of an unknown unit. Eastern front, 1944.

Sturmgeschütz IV prototype presented by *Krupp-Gruson AG* in December 1943. There is a Sturmgeschütz III Ausf. F/8 superstructure with a trapezoidal box-type gun mantlet installed on the *Panzerkampfwagen IV* chassis.

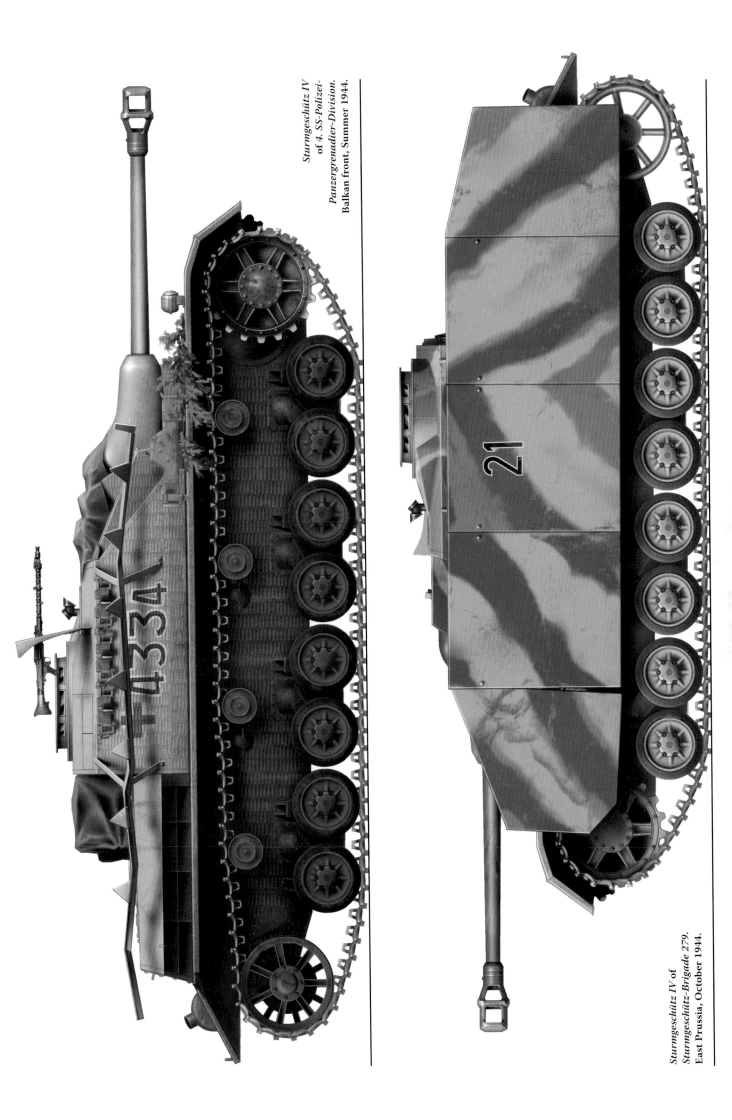

Sturmgeschütz IV
of 4. SS-Polizei-
Panzergrenadier-Division.
Balkan front, Summer 1944.

Sturmgeschütz IV of
Sturmgeschütz-Brigade 279.
East Prussia, October 1944.

Painted by Arkadiusz Wróbel

Sturmgeschütz IV of Panzer-Kompanie 1021. Gdynia (Gotenhafen), February 1945.

Early production series *Sturmgeschütz IV of Sturmgeschütz-Abteilung 1349. Tarnopol area, April 1944.*

KAGERO.EU

Messerschmitt Me 262 Schwalbe vol.

**Free magazines in download section
Kagero's Publication 2014 Catalogue**

Junkers Ju 87 D/G vol. I

READ FOR FREE
on KAGERO's Area

LIST OF PUBLICATION SERIES

TopColors

Messerschmitt Bf 109G Over Germany — Fighters over Japan — Eastern Front — Supermarine Spitfire Mk VIII — Messerschmitt Bf 109 F

miniTopColors   ## Units

Fw 190s over Europe — Captured Panzers German Vehicles in Allied Service — Pacific Lightnings — JG 26 Jagdgeschwader "Schlageter" — JG 53 "Pik As"

TopDrawings

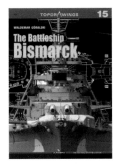  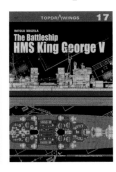 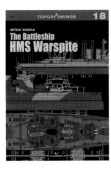 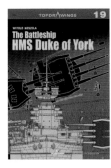 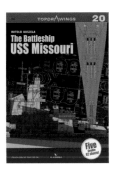

The Battleship Bismarck — Junkers Ju 88 bomber variants — The Battleship HMS King George V — The Battleship HMS Warspite — The Battleship HMS Duke of York — The Battleship USS Missouri

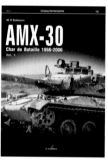

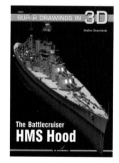
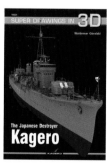
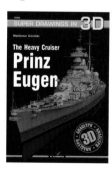
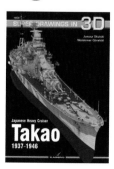
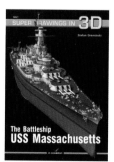
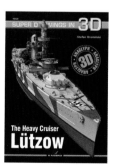